STAN BECKEN

ROCK CARVINGS
OF NORTHERN BRITAIN

SHIRE ARCHAEOLOGY

2

Cover photograph
This rock carving at Old Bewick, Northumberland, is a good example of
concentric cirles that flow into each other; ducts flow down
the rock, linking the figures.
(Photograph : Stan Beckensall.)

British Library Cataloguing in Publication Data available

Published by
SHIRE PUBLICATIONS LTD
Cromwell House, Church Street, Princes Risborough,
Aylesbury, Bucks HP17 9AJ, UK

Series Editor: James Dyer

ISBN 0 85263 760 8

First published 1986

Set in 11 point Times and printed in Great Britain by
C. I. Thomas & Sons (Haverfordwest) Ltd,
Press Buildings, Merlins Bridge, Haverfordwest, Dyfed.

Contents

4

List of illustrations

ORKNEY

MORAY

ABERDEEN

TAY

FORTH

NORTHUMBERLAND

ARGYLL

GALLOWAY

CUMBRIA
BARNINGHAM

N.E.YORKSHIRE

WEST YORKSHIRE

DERBYSHIRE

1. Map of northern Britain, showing the areas where rock carvings are found.

1
Introduction

The urge to paint on rock surfaces and to inscribe or peck naturalistic or symbolic pictures on them is almost universal, and prehistoric people in northern Britain carved a wide range of symbols on outcrop rock surfaces, boulders, small movable stones, standing stones and stones in burials.

This book covers Scotland and the north of England. Ireland's numerous carvings are different in many respects from those of Britain. The daggers and axes carved on uprights at Stonehenge are faint and isolated examples from the south, where there is an almost complete absence of prehistoric carving; Derbyshire marks the southern limit, with a few scattered carved rocks.

Text and bibliography refer to detailed works that in many cases are the result of the efforts of individuals who have found this study a neglected part of our heritage and a source of fascination. Not only are the places where the carvings are found often wild and beautiful, but the art form is a unique opportunity to explore a part of man's nature. It supplements what we know about life in the past and reaches into the spiritual part of existence.

The most common type of northern British rock carving is called *cup and ring,* a term that has been used since the study began in the nineteenth century. A *cup* is a depression made in the rock, varying in depth and radius, formed by picking at the rock with a tool, most probably made of hard rock. A *ring* is carved in the same way and commonly surrounds a cup, either by itself or with others arranged concentrically. 'Cups and rings' is a good, simple way of describing most of the carvings, but many are more complex than this and it is necessary to refer to the illustrations in order to understand them.

Most carvings are on outcrop rock that is usually horizontal or nearly so. It may have been exposed for centuries, or it may have been accidentally or deliberately uncovered recently.

Boulders, often rolled into place by glaciers, or sometimes moved into position by people, were also used. Some movable rocks with carvings have found their way into rockeries, dry stone walls, houses and other buildings. Others have been given to museums, used as hardcore, dumped at the sides of fields, or even blown up.

Whether the rocks remain *in situ* or have been moved, it is

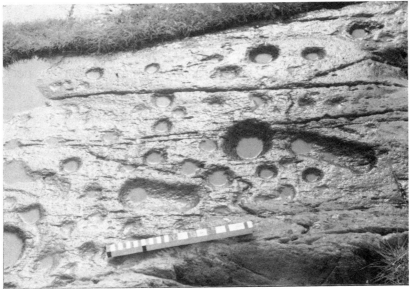

2. Cup marks and other carvings at Kilmartin Glassary, Argyll.

3. Weetwood Moor, Northumberland. *(Left)* A carving on a large kerbstone of a burial mound, which originally faced inward. *(Right)* A magnificent carving, one of many on flat outcrop rock. Scales in decimetres.

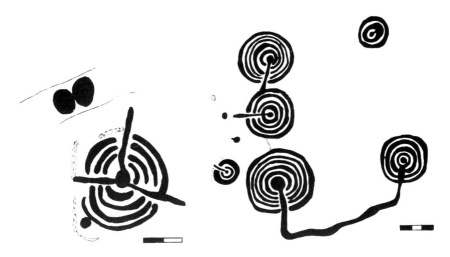

4. Chatton Park Hill, Northumberland. Carved on the largest rock, the central figure in this photograph is one of the most spectacular series of concentric circles in Britain. The additional cup and rings on the right are incorporated into the design, making it unique. The central cup is linked by a duct to the main channel that runs down the rock.

5. The 'tree of life' on Snowden Moor, West Yorkshire.

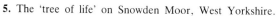

clear that all the carvers preferred the softer, sedimentary rocks. In Northumberland, for example, every example is on sandstone or gritstone. Greywacke was favoured in Galloway, and sandstones and gritstones in Yorkshire. Igneous and metamorphic rocks were generally avoided, presumably because it was hard to make an impression on them.

Of special importance are carvings that have been made on standing stones and in burials, for if we did not have these it would be impossible to date the carvings on outcrop rocks or speculate on their function.

The carvers belonged to a late neolithic and early bronze age culture, to communities who buried their dead in round barrows, who made beakers and food vessels, and whose main tools were of stone. In some areas this association is more obvious than in others; Northumberland, for example, has very little evidence of neolithic activity, but a strong tradition of carvings and round barrows. Most of the north-east Yorkshire carvings come from burial mounds, and in Scotland there are many decorated cist stones. It is the association of carvings with other finds that enables us not only to know who made them but to discover what they were for.

6. Simple markings (cups, some rings and ducts) on a standing stone at Nether Largie, Argyll.

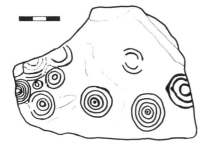

7. *(Above)* Cist cover from Craigie Hill, 9 kilometres (5½ miles) west of Edinburgh. *(Below)* Cist cover from Wester Yard-houses, near Carnwath, Lanarkshire, now in the Royal Museums of Scotland. Scales in decimetres.

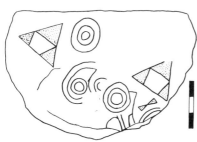

Although a detailed study of Irish sites is not possible here, we must be aware that in addition to cup-and-ring sites there is a tradition of passage grave art in which the passages, chambers and outside stones of the great Irish tombs are decorated with spirals, serpentine grooves, zigzags, 'sun' symbols and other shapes. These are known to be of an earlier date than English and Scottish sites, but the presence of similar forms among the more general cups and rings tends to blur the division. There is a link between Irish sites and the passage graves of the European Atlantic seaboard, but it is not known which are the earlier.

Excavated burial mounds in northern Britain have shown that small rocks with carvings were deliberately placed among other stones of the burial mound. The Hinderwell Beacon barrow in North Yorkshire is a classic example and is not the only one in that area. In Northumberland, excavations at Fowberry Moor and Weetwood revealed the same phenomenon and at Fowberry the double ring of retaining stones of a small cairn containing carved rocks was built over outcrop rock that had been covered with carvings.

Sometimes the kerbstones of burials have carvings. A 'four poster' at Goatstones (Northumberland), which Aubrey Burl regards as a structure dating to 1800 BC, has sixteen cups carved on one stone. At Weetwood (Northumberland) one barrow had a large peripheral stone carved with concentric circles and three radial grooves facing inward, deliberately obscured.

There are cup-marked stones in some Derbyshire barrows and in the Barningham Moor area near Barnard Castle, County Durham.

A rock shelter at Corby Crags (Northumberland) contained a cremation in a food vessel; the rock overhang has a basin, groove and duct carved on top, and a long groove is carved on the shelter floor.

Carvings on cists are particularly valuable in establishing associations with beaker and food vessel cultures. A cist is a stone-lined chest made specially for a burial. Some are empty when they are exposed, possibly because acidic soil has removed traces of the body. Many have contracted skeletons, flints, pots and occasionally ornaments in them. Some contain cremations. The size of the mound that covers these cists varies considerably, and the number of cists in one mound varies too.

Monuments to the dead have been numerous and have had a lucky survival rate, despite modern farming, mainly because they lie on land no longer of prime value to the farmer, although thousands must have been destroyed. Antiquaries of the past noted that some of the cists had carvings on them, either on the side slabs or on the capstone. The burials in some of these cists were accompanied by beakers and food vessels.

There is some evidence that a carving in a cist was made specifically for that purpose, where the pattern is complete, but

8. A stone deliberately buried in a mound at Fowberry, Northumberland, and showing peck marks. (Photograph: Museum of Antiquities of the University and Society of Antiquaries of Newcastle upon Tyne.)

9. A disturbed burial mound built over outcrop rock covered with carvings at Fowberry, Northumberland, and excavated by the author.

10. Cups, concentric circles and linking grooves on a rock on Barningham Moor, County Durham.

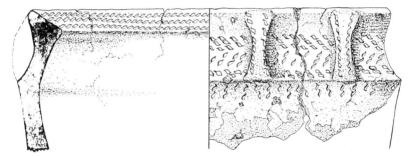

11. The remains of a food vessel buried under a rock overhang carved with a basin, groove and channel, at Corby Crags, Northumberland. (Drawing: Mary Hurrell.)

12. Temple Wood stone circle, Argyll. Some of the uprights and spacers have carvings, and the cairn includes a burial cist.

other carvings appear to have been broken before being used in the cist. At Bowes Museum there is a fine example of a cist cover carved on both sides, what presumably is the lower surface being carved with a simple and completely uneroded pick-marked pattern,and the rougher upper surface very elaborate. Usually only one surface was carved. A single cup mark inside a cist is of significance, as the act of making one was important to the people making the burial.

Patterns on cist slabs cover a wide range of motifs, but the Kilmartin (Argyll) barrow sites, where the axe appears, are unique. This motif is a representation of the metal expanding-

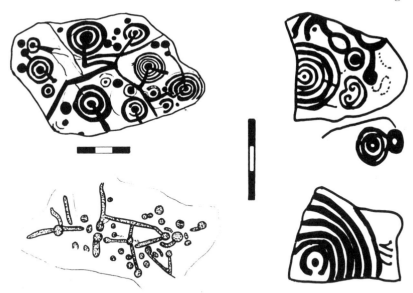

13. *(Above left)* A cist cover decorated on two sides, from Gainford, County Durham, now in the Bowes Museum, Barnard Castle. Scale in decimetres.
14. *(Above right)* Stones from Lilburn, Northumberland, the upper one buried with cremations. Scale in decimetres.
15. *(Below left)* Details of faint carvings on Long Meg, a standing stone near Great Salkeld, Cumbria, taken from rubbings. Scale in decimetres.
16. *(Below right)* A spiral linked to concentric circles on Little Meg, near Penrith, Cumbria. Scale in decimetres.

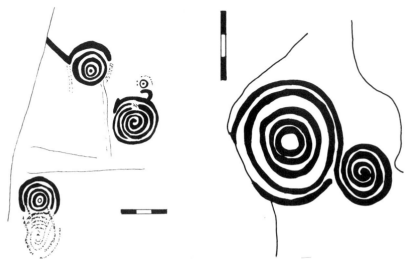

17. A spiral, one of two on the same upright at Temple Wood stone circle, Argyll.

edge type of axe. Only one spiral carving appears with burials, and this is at Lilburn (Northumberland), where a stone with spirals and cups and rings accompanied a unique series of cremation burials.

Small, simple cup marks in the structure of burial mounds may well have been overlooked during past excavations, and every stone must be carefully examined. The re-excavation of previously dug sites will probably add much more information.

The excavation of a henge monument at Milfield (Northumberland) discovered a cup-marked stone in a deep pit. The re-use of material from structures like barrows can lead to carved rocks being incorporated into walls, used as doorsteps, and such like. There must be many more lying around.

Some standing stones, either isolated or part of a circle or alignment, have carvings. Their function was related in some way to the function of the standing stones, but it is not possible to say in each case whether the carvings were made before the stones were erected, or how long after the stones were erected. Long Meg, for example, is a different kind of stone from her 'Daughters' (Cumbria) and could have been on the site before the erection of the stone circle or put there later. Yet it is possible to say that the decorating of standing stones with cups or cups and rings was part of a religious ritual. Professor Thom has pointed

Rock Carvings

18. A cist cover from High Auchenlarie, now at Kirkdale House,
Anwoth, Kirkcudbrightshire. It is a
fine example of a variety of designs on
one rock. Scale in decimetres.

out that in the Crinan Valley (Argyll) some important stones in
astronomical alignments have carvings. That area is worthy of
study, as the Temple Wood site has some fine spirals, concentric
circles and cups (the last now obscured) in what was an important
burial complex.

The outcrop rocks cannot be dated, but their position in
relation to burials and standing stones is significant.

It is not necessary to recount all the wild theories about the
purpose of these carvings. Anyone who wants to think that they
are pictures of sacred cowpats, messages from outer space or
adder lairs need read no more.

19. A lithograph by J. Collingwood Bruce of a carved rock from the island of Eday,
Orkney.

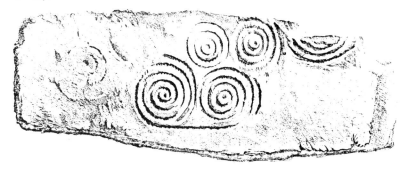

The indisputable evidence is that they are sacred or religious symbols, and they are the equivalent of a cross to a Christian. Why else would they appear carved on cists and even on the small stones that make up burial cairns? Why should cups, rings, spirals and other symbols be used for the great passage graves? They are not maps, pictures or family trees; they are symbols, and there is nothing to be gained by guessing what they symbolise. The fact that they are abstractions and not naturalistic depictions of people or animals or buildings (as some carvings are in other countries) makes them even more fascinating and mysterious.

As works of art they are interesting in their own right, and as symbols they expressed an idea that could not be expressed in any other way. The individuality of the carvers is heartening, for they managed to produce some interesting variations in a very limited symbolism with the use of limited materials. Probably the act of making them was an important part of their purpose, and the choice of suitable rock surfaces (not the best for carving in some cases) must have been determined by considerations now lost to us.

One of the first rock carvings to be recognised was the Old Bewick rock (Northumberland), in the 1820s. Since then a number of antiquarians, including George Tate, J. Y. Simpson and J. Collingwood Bruce, have done pioneering work, which has culminated in some good pieces of detailed and general work,

20. A rubbing of carvings from Achnabreck, Argyll.

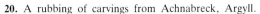

21. The Beanley cist cover from Northumberland. Length: 35 inches (90 cm).

22. The Cochno stone, from near Glasgow. (Drawing by R. W. B. Morris and reproduced with his kind permission.)

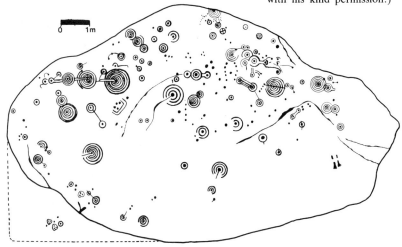

23. Two carvings of particular interest from Northumberland: *(right)* from Dod Law; *(below)* from West Horton. Scales in decimetres.

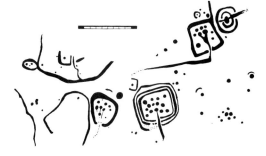

24. Amerside Law Moor, Northumberland. This important carving includes the rare motif of a rectangle within a rectangle as well as an arc of linked cups.

25. Fowberry Enclosure, Northumberland: a unique small grid of twenty small squares and other figures that are 'pecked'.

with archaeologists such as Ronald W. B. Morris to the forefront. The first job of the recorder is to record accurately what he sees. In the nineteenth century there were some impressive lithographs, and other illustrations, but not all recording corresponds to what we see in the field today. This is either because the recording was not thorough enough, or because subsequent erosion of the rock surface has made a difference.

Today we have good cameras, but good results depend upon choosing the right time of day at which to photograph the carvings, especially as some marks are faint. This necessitates many visits to a site, often at different times of the year.

There are many other ways of recording. Making a wax rubbing of the whole rock, checking with photographs, and transferring the results to an accurate scale drawing via a polythene sheet divided into decimetre squares is recommended.

26. Spirals and other features on a cliff at Morwick, Northumberland.

27. A small outcrop carving just south of the boundary fence at Rimside Moor, Northumberland.

Care has to be taken in cleaning the surface of the rock. A drawing and photograph together are better than words.

Rocks that are newly excavated should receive treatment of the highest standard in excavation technique, cleaning and recording. The problem then arises of what to do with them. A replica could be made but this is very expensive. To re-cover the rock would preserve it, but no one would then be able to see it. However, if the rock is in danger of being damaged there may be no alternative. If the rock is not to be covered up, it has to be decided whether it should be fenced, perhaps with noticeboards added, or left open, vulnerable to the elements and to vandalism, but better preserving the atmosphere of the site and retaining it as it was meant to be seen. Each case has to be taken on its own merits.

Luckily, there has been a surge of international interest in prehistoric rock carvings, and there has been an expansion in publication of the sites.

The sites are too numerous to list in full, but there follows a general account of each region, describing the best and most accessible sites and museums. Those who require more detail should refer to the works listed in the bibliography. Sites of rock carvings are given in **bold** type, while the sources of carvings now kept elsewhere, such as in museums, are printed in *italic* type.

2
Derbyshire

Ordnance Survey 1:50,000 sheet 119.

John Barnatt's paper in *Derbyshire Archaeological Journal* C11 (1982) gives details of rock carvings in the county, and his book on stone circles and henges in the same region has useful information and maps of a more general nature.

The millstone grit moorlands on either side of the river Derwent are the most productive area, but overall there are few sites. Some carvings appear on outcrop rocks and boulders, but those associated with burials and stone circles add more to our knowledge of their purpose.

Sheffield City Museum, Weston Park, Sheffield.

Some Derbyshire and Peak District stones are at Sheffield City Museum: *Gardom's Edge* slab, found near an outcrop carving; *Bleakley Dike* slab, found in a stream; *Burr Tor* slab, carved on both sides in a 'passage grave' tradition; three stones from the ditch of a small hillfort of the late bronze age and early iron age at *Ball Cross*; four carved slabs from *Barbrook* barrow; two cup-marked stones from a barrow at *Brund* (Staffordshire), associated with a cremation; a cup-marked stone found in a barrow at *Elkstone* with a cremation, a burnt flint and knife and a pot.

Stones still on their sites. At **Gardom's Edge** (SK 2730 7301) there is a good outcrop that has been recovered. At **Stanage Barrow,** Eyam (SK 2154 7865), a decorated slab that may be a disturbed cist cover is sticking out of a disturbed barrow.

The **Barbrook II stone circle** (SK 2775 7582) has a small carved slab that was a cist cover inside the ring cairn, and a kerbstone of the small internal cairn has a single cup on its upper edge. The cairn contained a collared urn and cremation of 1500 ± 150 BC, two burnt scrapers and a flint knife.

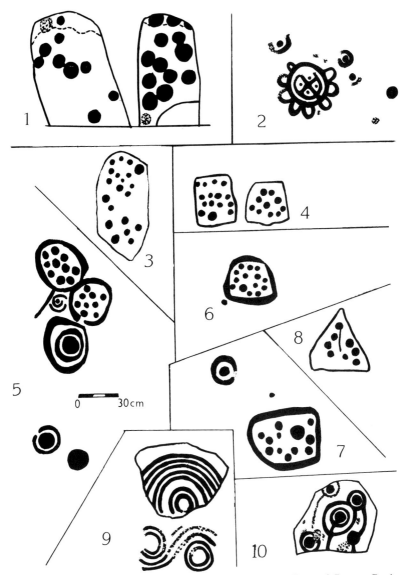

28. Some of the Derbyshire rock carvings: 1 Stanage Barrow, Eyam; 2 Rowtor Rocks, Birchover; 3 Bleakley Dike; 4 Barbrook II stone circle; 5 Gardom's Edge; 6 Gardom's Edge; 7 Ball Cross; 8 Ball Cross; 9 Burr Tor; 10 Calton Pasture. (Based on the work of John Barnatt, with his kind permission.)

3
West Yorkshire

Ordnance Survey 1:50,000 sheet 104.

Since Arthur Raistrick's work on West Yorkshire, a great deal of fieldwork has been done. Prominent in this has been Stuart Feather, as well as a group of enthusiastic amateurs that includes Anne Haig, Dr Keith Boughey and Bill Godfrey.

The West Yorkshire group is furthest inland, and the flat outcrops of millstone grit have a variety of themes and treatment.

29. Map of sites in West Yorkshire. The circles denote cups and rings.

30. Part of the Panorama Stone at Ilkley, West Yorkshire. The ladder design is restricted to this area.

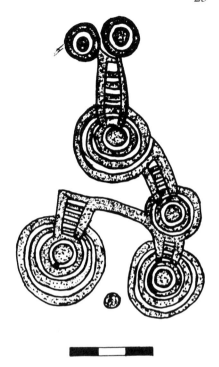

Ilkley Moor

The **Hanging Stones,** near the Cow and Calf Hotel, are easily accessible by road and path (SE 1281 4675). Opposite St Mary's church (SE 115473) are pieces of the **Panorama Stone,** cut away from their home, inside railings,and they have the Ilkley 'ladder' motif, unique to the Ilkley area, leading away from the central cup and circles. This motif is repeated on the north moor on the **Barmishaw** stone (SE 1190 4642). In contrast to this design is the **Pepperpot Rock,** White Wells (SE 1180 4654), where the rock surface is covered with cups. The **Idol Stone** (SE 1326 4595) brings a regimented discipline to cups by putting them in rows and separating them by long grooves; this rock lies at Green Crag Slack, where the carving emphasises cups rather than the elaborate patterns found to the north of the moor. **Backstone Beck** (SE 1277 4625) also has an emphasis on cups, but grooves and an occasional ring make the stone impressive.

31. A carving on Snowden Moor, West Yorkshire.

32. A carved rock at Dobrudden caravan site, Baildon Moor, West Yorkshire.

The **Badger Stone** is well worth a visit (SE 1105 4606), and so is the **Pipers Crag Stone** on Addingham Moor (SE 0847 4710), carved in concentric circles before the rock drops away abruptly to the north.

It is doubtful whether the **Swastika Stone** belongs to the same tradition of carving as all the others, but is accessible in its fenced-in enclose on Woodhouse Crag (SE 094470).

At **Rivock Edge** there is a good variety in design, including the use of vertical and horizontal lines, but for the casual visitor there are difficulties finding the carvings, since the area has been planted and they are on private land.

On Ilkley Moor there is no connection between carvings and other monuments such as burials or standing stones, and it would be very difficult to guess the purpose or time-scale of the carvings without reference to other areas.

Baildon Moor

Baildon Moor can be reached from Bingley and Shipley, and there is an accessible group near the north wall of **Dobrudden Farm** caravan park. One stone, now upright, has cups that have been 'zoned' with grooves.

Snowden Moor

On Snowden Moor possibly the best carving is the one known as 'The Tree of Life' (SE 1800 5110), in which cups have been linked to a central groove to produce a fine design.

The Chevin

On The Chevin a few small carved rocks have been reported.

4
The Barnard Castle area and northern Yorkshire Dales

Ordnance Survey 1:50,000 sheet 99.

The Bowes Museum, Barnard Castle, County Durham.
At the Bowes Museum in Barnard Castle there are three carved rocks of considerable interest. Inside the museum is a perfect little carving from a wall near *Dalton* village (where there is another in a private garden). There is also a splendid rock carved on both sides, a cist cover that came from *Gainford,* showing considerable contrast between the simple cup-and-groove pecked pattern on one side and the elaborate zoning and multiple concentric circles on the other, rougher side. In the grounds near the south wall to the east of the main gate is a large flat slab from *Greta Bridge,* where it was found during widening of the A66 road, a quarter of a mile (400 m) east of the Roman

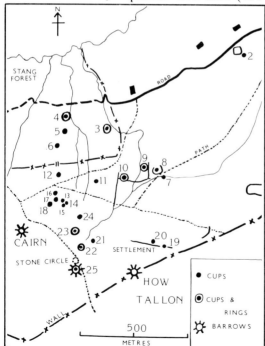

33. Map of sites on Barningham Moor, County Durham. (Based on a map by T. C. Laurie.)

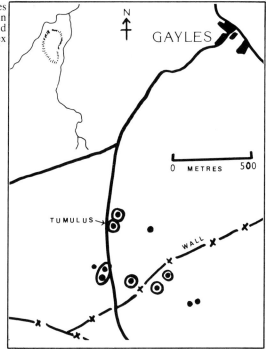

34. Map of sites on Gayles Moor, North Yorkshire. Plain dots represent cup-marked stones, ringed dots complex carvings.

fort. It had been re-used as the cover of a Roman burial. It has simple cup marks and a deep, bent groove linking the cups. The pick marks are fresh.

At nearby **Egglestone Abbey** is another carved rock, above the north bank of the Thorsgill Beck (NZ 0612 1521).

Barningham Moor

The intensive fieldwork of Mr T. C. Laurie has led to the discovery of twenty-six carved rocks on this grouse preserve that forms the southern edge of the Tees valley 6 miles (10 km) due south of Barnard Castle (centre at NZ 058083).

Many carvings are on small earthfast rocks, several within stone-banked enclosures, and one protruding from a barrow.

There is on the summit of **Eel Hill** a fallen standing stone, number 23, with a clearly pecked basin, 250 millimetres (10 inches) deep, cups and rings. It lies on the major axis of a small stone circle at the head of Osmonds Gill. Near the stone circle is a barrow with a cup-marked and grooved stone protruding from the top. Osmonds Gill is a beautiful, peaceful place, with a line of

35. *(Left)* Carvings from Barningham Moor; the numbers refer to the map (fig. 33). The unnumbered carving, from Dalton, North Yorkshire, is at the Bowes Museum, Barnard Castle.
36. *(Right)* A carved rock from Greta Bridge, County Durham, now at the Bowes Museum, Barnard Castle.

small standing stones at the head of the valley, flanked by stone number 22, among the scree.

Swaledale

There are no sites in the main valley of Swaledale; however, above the Marske Beck at **Skelton Moor** (NZ 085002 and 081019) are two sites with miniature cups and grooves and cups and rings. They are close to field walls attached to prehistoric parallel land divisions (reaves), which extend over an area of 9 square kilometres (3½ square miles). The reaves, a very interesting discovery by Mr Laurie, are fully described by him in *Upland Settlement in Britain* (British Archaeological Reports, edited by Don Spratt and Colin Burgess).

A third site at **Holgate How** (NZ 067042) has cups, rings and branching grooves.

Gayles Moor

Gayles Moor is an army range and is accessible only at certain

37. A carving lying just west of the road at Gayles Moor, North Yorkshire.
38. A fallen stone with carvings at Barningham Moor, County Durham.

times. The carvings easiest to reach lie close to the road from the village of Gayles and cluster near a large burial mound ('howe') covered with young trees.

The map shows the sites in a limited area. Other rocks have been noted by Mr Stuart Feather in the Yorkshire Archaeological Register but not all can now be found and some are either buried or lost under heather.

The rocks are well worth a visit and include many cups, rings, grooves and shallow basins.

Wensleydale

The only cup-marked site is the summit cairn on **Addlebrough** (SD 946882), a prominent hill 1½ miles (2.4 km) south-east of Bainbridge. Several large kerbstones have multiple cups.

5
North-east Yorkshire and Cleveland

Ordnance Survey 1:50,000 sheets 94, 101.

Dr D. A. Spratt's book *Prehistoric and Roman Archaeology of North-East Yorkshire* (British Archaeological Reports 104, 1982) is a comprehensive review of the area. Not only are all the sites listed, but there is valuable comment on factors affecting land and population. The bibliography and maps are good, but there are no pictures of carvings.

In prehistoric times in north-east Yorkshire the high sandstone moors were being destroyed with the advance of pastoral and arable farming, and settlements were eventually concentrated on rich lowland, particularly in limestone areas. No doubt these richer areas were always favoured, and prime agricultural sites have been so heavily farmed that evidence of previous agriculture and communities has been ploughed out, whereas the moorlands today can preserve prehistoric monuments such as barrows, cairnfields and enclosures. Even so, in recent times there has

39. Map of sites in north-east Yorkshire and Cleveland.

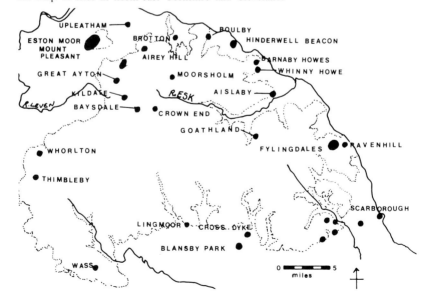

40. Carvings found in a tumulus near Scarborough and described by John Tissiman in 1852.

been encroachment on marginal land in many parts of northern Britain, and consequent destruction of the prehistoric past.

This region has cup marks and cups and rings, notably associated with burial mounds, and some associated with enclosures. As elsewhere, carvings on outcrop rock cannot be dated, but the association of carvings with beakers and food vessels gives us an early bronze age context. With very few exceptions, the carvings are found in regions on the periphery of the hills, the most favoured settlement areas. The high moorlands, although having a spread of burials and cairns (many from field clearances), do not seem to be places where people lived permanently, nor was there much funerary activity there. One exception is the appearance of cup and ring stones in a small cairn on **Near Moor,** Whorlton (SE 474998). The piles of stones, lynchets, hollow ways and elaborate systems of field walls (needed as stockades and to keep the animals off the crops) are the work of farmers who practised mixed farming and eventually ruined soil fertility. There are cup-and-ring stones in the wall at Near Moor, where a large round barrow is also incorporated in the wall. This occurrence of carved stones in enclosure walls is repeated on Barningham Moor (see chapter 4).

The pushing of pastures into the hill forests for seasonal mixed farming, to supplement whatever other farming was going on in richer areas, ruined the thin soil. In this area there were no central places of ceremony, and barrows mark the places where local leaders of segmented tribes held sway.

The map shows how the sites of carvings lie on the edges of the high moorland, coinciding with finds of beakers and food vessels. Most of the carvings were found during the excavation of barrows, some of which were very prolific: Hinderwell Beacon, for example, produced 150 carvings. Such discoveries conform with similar ones in Northumberland.

The **Hinderwell Beacon** was a mound enclosed by a stone circle about 30 feet (9.1 m) in diameter with a 4 feet (1.2 m) thick wall. It contained seven cremations, two with food vessels. A third vessel stood by the side of an urn with calcined bones. 150 stones had one, two, three and four cups, one other having an incised cross and another a V shape. This indicates that the actual carving of a cup mark had religious significance and was offered to the dead as part of the covering structure.

Other barrows contained cup stones in the mound: several at **Boulby** (NZ 745190); twenty-four cups and one cup and ring at **Howe Hill,** Brotton (NZ 695189); one at **Street Houses** (NZ 736196) and at **Eston Hills** (NZ 574184). Some barrow kerbstones had carvings: nineteen cups and three grooves at **Upleatham** (NZ 624202); six cups at **Airey Hill** (NZ 644167). There were cups on barrow kerbs at **Barnby Howes** (NZ 830138) and thirty at **Moorsholm** (NZ 691120). Canon Greenwell, famous for his extensive excavations in the nineteenth century, reported many cup stones in three excavated barrows on Wass Moor.

A cup-and-ring stone with a beaker came from **Mount Pleasant** (NZ 558165), cup stones with a food vessel from **Whinney Howe** (NZ 833145), one with a handled beaker from **Guisborough**. Six cup-marked stones were associated with urns and an axe hammer at **Ling Moor** (SE 713883), others with food vessels and urns at **Hutton Buscel** (SE 959872), and with beaker and urn sherds at **Blansby Park** (SE 814865).

There are carvings on outcrop rock at **Eston Hills** (NZ 564174), **Aislaby** (NZ 658091), **Baysdale** (NZ 623068) and **Allan Tofts** (NZ 829030). Mr Stuart Feather has recorded seventeen outcrop carvings with cups, cups and rings and other symbols at **Fylingdales** (NZ 963018 to NZ 952004). A boulder at **Thimbleby Moor** (SE 460960) is cup-marked.

Other carvings come from drystone walls, dykes, a hillfort ditch and the floor of an iron age hut — a pattern of finds similar to that in Northumberland.

6
Northumberland

Ordnance Survey 1:50,000 sheets 75, 81.

It was in Northumberland, at Old Bewick, that the study of carvings began and since the 1820s the number of known sites has grown, making this one of the richest and most varied areas.
Most of the carvings appear on horizontal and near-horizontal outcrop rocks, all sandstone, mainly on the Fell sandstone scarplands, in places which command extensive views. There are many sites to visit with a great variety of design. Of particular interest are the Fowberry and Weetwood barrows, which demonstrate the purpose of the carvings, and the carving on the rock shelter at Corby Crags, and the outcrop rocks are in some cases very large.
All the sites but two are 'cup-and-ring' types, but at Morwick there are spirals carved on a cliff rising from the river Coquet, and a series of cremation burials dug out in the nineteenth century at Lilburn produced a good spiral-decorated and cup-and-ring stone.
There are rectangular and heart-shaped patterns among the carvings, rosette patterns, pear-shaped concentric grooves and serpentine grooves. Almost every variation appears here, including a 'grid'. Some of the most interesting and important sites are described below.

Roughting Linn (NT 9839 3674) is a huge rock easily accessible off the Wooler to Berwick road, with a variety of carvings ranging from deep, large cups, rings and grooves to delicate flower-like stems. It is the largest carved rock in northern England and well worth a visit.

Dod Law (main rock at NU 0049 3173) **Gled Law** (various rocks, with two particularly good ones at NU 0103 3066 and 0121 3087), **Buttony** (NU 0172 3103) and **West Horton** (NU 0214 3155) are all in the same general area and can be reached from a number of directions. The carvings are spectacular. Originally there were burial mounds, but these have been cleared away. A golf course marks the Dod Law site. There are some fine hillforts and enclosures. Doddington is the nearest village.

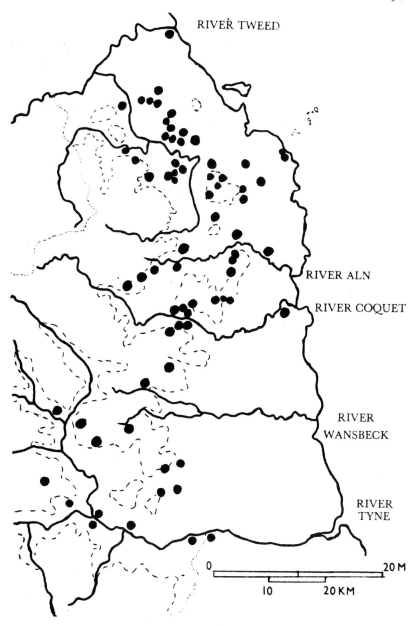

41. The distribution of rock carvings in Northumberland.

42. Northumberland: locations of the main sites referred to in the text.

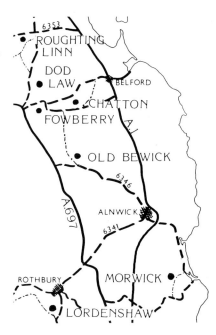

43. Roughting Linn, Northumberland, one of the largest carved rocks in Britain.

metre

44. Dod Law, Northumberland, a very impressive rock.

45. Buttony, Northumberland: concentric circles and radial grooves.

46. Buttony, Northumberland: concentric circles and a diametric groove. Scale in inches.

47. Rock carvings at Weetwood Moor, Northumberland.

48. Fowberry barrow site, Northumberland, excavated by the author. Scale in inches.

Weetwood and **Fowberry** (NU 0197 2784 and 0215 2810). There are two burial mounds that the writer has excavated and reconstructed, and many fine carvings on horizontal outcrop rock.

Chatton Park Hill (NU 0757 2906). Accessible from the Wooler to Belford road, there are large outcrop rocks with concentric circles, domino cups, rectangles and channels.

Old Bewick (NU 0781 2158). A large block of stone with carvings is the focal point, and well worth the walk from the road. There are another eight carvings around the main one. In 1984 an excavation of the Blawearie cairns revealed vertical picking on kerbstones. One kerbstone had picked-out cup marks.

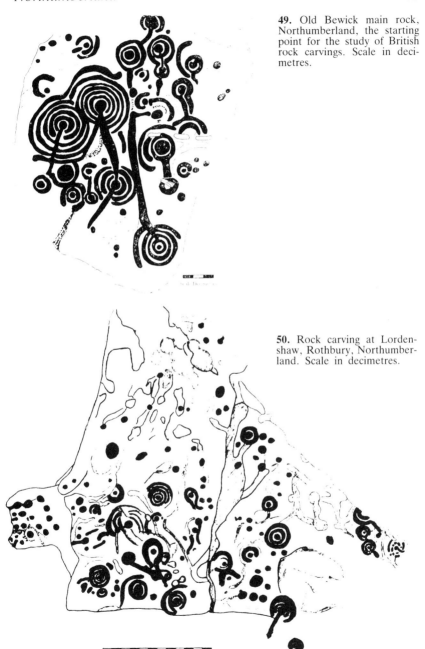

49. Old Bewick main rock, Northumberland, the starting point for the study of British rock carvings. Scale in decimetres.

50. Rock carving at Lordenshaw, Rothbury, Northumberland. Scale in decimetres.

Lordenshaw, Rothbury (several sites: main rock to the west at NZ 0523 9914 and to the east NZ 0585 9965). There is a contrast here with other sites, with an emphasis on very big cups, basins and enormous channels, making it a very distinctive region. Many cup marks are on burial mounds. The sites are easily reached to the west of the Rothbury to Hexham road, the centre of the complex being a hillfort.

Morwick, Warkworth (NU 2326 0441). There is only one other site like this, at Hawthornden near Edinburgh. Spirals and cups and rings are carved on the cliff face. The site is reached, awkwardly, via Morwick Mill.

Other carvings.

Although the Museum of Antiquities of the University and the Society of Antiquaries of Newcastle upon Tyne has many fine stones, none is on display. There is a good stone at St John Lee church, **Acomb,** near Hexham, and one at *Corstopitum* Roman site, **Corbridge. Alnwick Castle Museum** has two good cist covers and an interesting collection of other prehistoric material.

Full details of all the Northumberland sites are given in the author's *The Prehistoric Carved Rocks of Northumberland* and *Northumberland's Prehistoric Rock Carvings*.

51. A stone in Tullie House Museum, Carlisle, from Honey Pots Farm, Edenhall, Penrith, Cumbria. Scale in decimetres.

7
Cumbria

Ordnance Survey 1:50,000 sheet 91.

The visitor may most profitably visit **Tullie House Museum,** Castle Street, Carlisle, and two sites called Long Meg and Little Meg. The stones, two *in situ*, are in the Penrith area and are accessible from the road linking Langwathby, Little Salkeld, Glassonby and Kirkoswald east of the Eden valley.

A whinstone boulder from *Honey Pots Farm,* where it was found in 1909 near a drystone wall, is now displayed at Tullie House Museum.

At Great Salkeld is **Long Meg and Her Daughters** (NY 572372), a fine stone circle outside which stands a pillar of red sandstone with spiral and cup and ring carvings. It is impossible to say how the carvings relate to the erection of the stone or to its position outside the circle, but it was certainly chosen because it was outstanding. The carvings are faint and need strong lights in which to view them.

Less well known is **Little Meg** (NY 577375), the remains of eleven stones that once surrounded a cist, now uncared for on the side of a field. There is a finely carved boulder still visible, with a spiral linked to five concentric circles, clearly pecked. It is also known as the Maughanby Stone. Found here also were a smaller sandstone with cups and rings, taken to Penrith Museum, Middlegate, Penrith, and a semi-ovoid cist that once held an urn and cremation burial; some of the stones were reported to have had markings like those on Long Meg.

The **Glassonby** stone circle and tumulus (NY 573393) had four concentric circles and two groups of U-shaped figures attached, very like those in Ireland and Gavrinis (Brittany).

A tumulus at Old Parks, Kirkoswald, before it was systematically destroyed for road metal, was 80 by 63 feet (24 by 19 m) in diameter and included carvings unlike the usual cups and rings. This and other sites are reported in *The Transactions of the Cumberland and Westmorland Antiquarian and Archaeological Society.*

8
The Edinburgh area

Ordnance Survey 1:50,000 sheets 65, 66.

There are a great many individual carved stones in Scotland, so the reader is directed to a selected number of sites. This is not to deny that many scattered individual stones are of great interest. Fortunately, the Royal Museums of Scotland, Queen Street, Edinburgh, have a very fine collection of stones from all over Scotland, many of which are from burials.

CARVINGS IN THE ROYAL MUSEUMS OF SCOTLAND
Each stone listed below is given the museum's reference number and arranged under its region. Notes point out any particular significance of the find. All numbers have the prefix 1A, unless stated otherwise.

Borders
Drumdelzier (41): four double rings and a single ring on a slab that came from a cairn with a cist, beaker, burial urns, and parts of a jet armlet.
Harelawside, Duns (47): a smooth greenstone boulder with cup and two rings and incised lines.
Kalemouth, Roxburgh (48): a small gritstone boulder with cup, four rings and two parallel grooves from the inner ring, found near to a cairn.
Lamancha, Peebles (6): a red sandstone slab found in a gravel bank with four double rings and parts of five double rings, a horned spiral, one with three convolutions, one with one.

Central
Torwood, or *Tapproch Broch,* Denny (GM 36-8): three carved gritstone slabs found in the tumbled stones of a broch, bearing simple cups and rings.

Dumfries and Galloway
Bardriston (43): cast with cup, duct and concentric circles.
Barrholm Hill, Gatehouse of Fleet (40): cast of a cup, duct and two circles now at Kirkdale House.
Cairnholy 1 (EO 830) : this is from an important site — a neolithic long barrow with two chambers. A secondary (later)

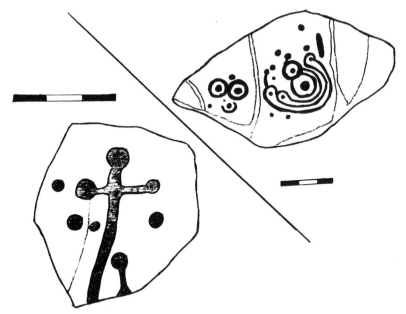

52. Two carvings at Tormain Hill, Lothian.

insertion contained this greywacke slab with a cup and six rings. It accompanied a food vessel.

Cairnholy (38): a cast of a cup and three rings of a rock now under turf.

Gallows Outon, Whithorn (27): a cast of an S-shaped spiral, *High Banks,* Kirkcudbright (16-19) : these are casts of some of the carvings, described in chapter 9.

Laggan (Kirkdale House) (42): cast of a small stone (drawn in chapter 9).

Mossyard, Anwoth (33): a greywacke slab built into a wall. Cup, duct, five rings (flattened), and groove linking three cups.

Redbrae, Wigtown (45) : this roughly hexagonal greywacke cist cover has a hole bored through it, cups and incised lines.

Fife
Balbirnie : see chapter 12.
Wemyss Caves (35, 271, 273): these are casts of carvings found in the caves.

Grampian

Cabrach (48): cup and four gapped rings, with duct from inner ring.

Cunnington (36, 37): parts of a cup and three rings; slab with three incomplete concentric rings.

Forgue (34): six cups and one gapped ring; three cups.

Lothian

Blackford Hill (34): a boulder carved on both sides with cups and rings and a duct from a cup.

Braid Hills (29): a white sandstone boulder carved with cups, rings and ducts.

Kaimes Hill (50-6): the casts are, unusually, of carvings on basalt.

Parkburn Quarry (49): a sandstone slab from a cist cemetery that has been quarried away is the side slab of a cist that contained a food vessel and skeleton. The stone may have been re-used after the carving was made.

Traprain Law, East Linton (GV 97-8, 289-294) : the carvings, some of them casts, came from a hillside outcrop, now quarried away. Unusually, they are incised, not pecked, and there is some hatching. It is not possible to say when they were carved, as the site has been used for centuries.

Orkney

Eday (2): two spirals of four and five convolutions, two cups and three rings, one with part of a fourth, and three concentric circles.

Pickaquoy (3): cup, three complete rings, and part of a fourth.

Redland (4): four concentric circles.

Stenness (44) : four possible cups, one with a ring.

Strathclyde

Cairnbaan 3, Argyll (7): this western end-slab of a cist has five concentric lozenges and part of a sixth. It is like 'passage grave' art or part of the metalwork in the famous Bush Barrow.

Ri Cruin, Kilmartin, Argyll (12-13) : casts of the end-slab of a cist that has axe carvings, and an end-slab with ten lines projecting from a long groove (the original is now lost).

Wester Yardhouses, Carnwath, Lanarkshire (EQ116): a very interesting gritstone found in a cist (figure 7). The illustration shows that it is in the Irish 'passage grave' tradition, and the two triangles are unique in Scotland. A beaker was found in the cist.

Tayside
Cargill (26) : three cups and one gapped ring, ducts, five cups.
Letham Grange (5): cist cover carved on both sides; cups, rings, ducts.
Williamston (20): two cups, one gapped ring, nineteen cups.

SITES IN LOTHIAN
The following sites are within reach of Edinburgh, and reasonably accessible:

Bonnington Mains, Tormain Hill (NT 1290 6966) : 875 yards (800 m) north-east of the farm, 8½ miles (13.5 km) west of Edinburgh, are exposed patches of outcrop rock, where there are five sites close together. One has cups linked to form a cross.

Glencorse church (NT 246628): a red standstone decorated slab lies against the church tower.

The Grange, Linlithgow (NT 000788) : the summerhouse has a flat stone with cups and rings.

Hawthornden (NT 2802 6324): this site is a cliff 164 yards (150 m) west of Gorton House, 6¾ miles (11 km) south of Edinburgh, 26 feet (8 m) above the river Esk and 100 yards (90 m) downstream from Wallace's cave. Of particular interest are the spirals, similar to some at Morwick, Northumberland. The site is difficult to reach.

9
Galloway

Ordnance Survey 1:50,000 sheets 83, 84.

For further information about this area see *The Prehistoric Rock Art of Galloway and the Isle of Man*, by Ronald W. B. Morris. The following is a selection of sites, in an order in which it is suggested they could be visited.

Balcraig 1 and 2 (NX 337444 and NX 373440). Balcraig 1 is 600 metres (650 yards) north-west of Balcraig Farm, in an enclosure fence. The greywacke slab has some well carved ungapped concentric circles, one with nine rings and one small spiral.

Balcraig 2, also enclosed, is 600 metres (650 yards) west of the farm in Near Windlestraw Field, 120 metres (130 yards) off the B7021 and 270 metres (300 yards) east of a wood. There are good concentric circles, one figure with nine rings, and in one case a duct going uphill. Lichen and moss obscure some of the carvings.

Drumtrodden (NX 362447). 200 metres (220 yards) south of the farm are fenced outcrops. There are many cups and rings visible, all easily accessible.

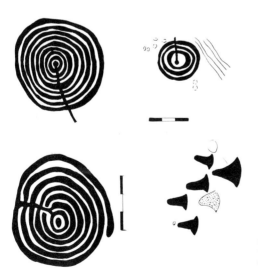

53. Four Scottish rock carvings. *(Top)* Two from Balcraig, Galloway. *(Bottom left)* A spiral from Cauldside Burn, Kirkcudbright. *(Bottom right)* Axe heads carved on the end slab of a cist at Ri Cruin, Argyll. Scales in decimetres.

54. Carved rocks at Drumtrodden, Galloway.
55. Carvings at Broughton Mains, Galloway.

Broughton Mains 1 and 2 (NX 4581 4565 and NX 452453). Both sites are on private land; both are well worth a visit. The first outcrop, a slight ridge in the middle of a field 850 metres (930 yards) north-east of the farm, has some very interesting carvings, but their accessibility depends on what the field is being used for. Visitors should check with the farmer.

The second site, 300 metres (330 yards) west-northwest of the farm, 100 metres (110 yards) north-east of the road's thorn hedge, consists of two large greywacke slabs covered with cups and rings and an unusual incised 'ladder'.

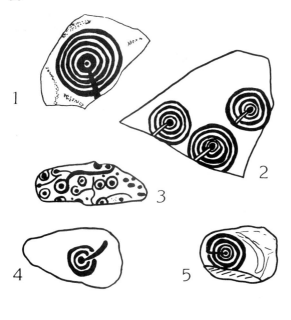

56. A collection of carved rocks at Kirkdale House, Anwoth, Kirkcudbrightshire : 1 Cardroness Estate; 2 Laggan; 3 Upper Newton; 4 Barholm; 5 Laggan. Scale in decimetres.

Kirkdale House, Anwoth (NX 515533). To the west of the house is a shed, built to house six carved rocks and two early Christian crosses, all of which came from the Cardroness Estate. The carvings are: 1, *Barholm,* a small slab; 2, *High Auchenlarie 2,* a possible cist cover — one of the best in Scotland because it has so many different designs; 3, *Laggan 2,* possibly part of a cist — the double ducts leading from the centre are an interesting feature; 4, *Laggan 3,* found in a wall almost opposite Cairnholy chambered tomb; 5, *Upper Newton Farm*; 6, provenance unknown — it was built into a sundial and bears very distinct pick marks.

Cairnholy 1 and 2 (NX 5177 5389). 250 metres (270 yards) south of the farm, Cairnholy 1 is an excavated chambered tomb of the neolithic period, but a secondary burial cist contained a slab with six concentric circles around a cup, and its capstone (still on site) has faint cups and rings. The slab is in the Royal Museums of Scotland, Queen Street, Edinburgh. The second chambered tomb, further along the track, is very impressive.

57. The 'Prince of Wales's Feathers' carving at Torrs, Galloway. Scale in decimetres.

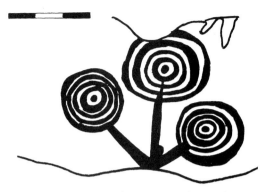

Cambret Moor (NX 528574). 1500 metres (1640 yards) north-east of Cambret, 295 metres (320 yards) north-northwest of the neolithic Cauldside Cairn, this takes time to reach, but it is a fine six-convolution spiral on a greywacke slab.

The Stewartry Museum, St Mary Street, Kirkcudbright, has a slab from *Blackmyre* (NX 497570) found in a farm wall, a fine slab from *Laggan* with multiple concentric circles, cup and duct, and casts of the *High Banks* carvings.

58. The carving of cups and grooves at Torrs, Galloway.

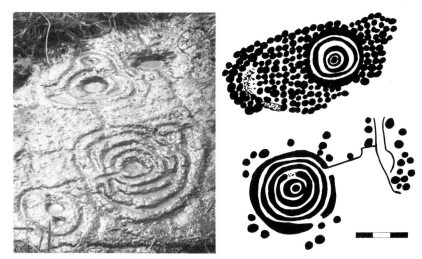

59. *(Left)* Carvings at Townhead Farm, near Kirkcudbright.
60. *(Right)* Some of the carvings at High Banks, Galloway. Scale in decimetres.

Torrs 1 and 2 (NX 6802 4586 and 6805 4586). The carvings lie on outcrops 15 metres (16 yards) to the north of the farm among some untidy land. The first is an unusual arrangement of cups and grooves. The second (called the 'Prince of Wales's Feathers') is three sets of four concentric circles around cups. The two carvings are 26 metres (28 yards) apart.

Townhead 1-3 (NX 6932 4718, 6847 4712, 6941 4713). Townhead Farm is 4.5 kilometres (2¾ miles) south-southeast of Kirkcudbright. The sites are close enough together to see at one visit. The starting point is 55 metres (60 yards) east of the gate into the third field along a track north-northwest of the farm 950 metres (1040 yards) away.

High Banks (NX 709489). The carvings here are unique and spectacular, and it is well worth the effort of leaving the metalled road to find them. The site is on an outcrop ridge 400 metres (440 yards) south-east of the farm, bounded by two walls, 30 metres (33 yards) north-east and 108 metres (118 yards) west-northwest. The most interesting is a natural 'bolster' with concentric circles around a cup that is the centre of a mass of cup marks.

10
Argyll

Ordnance Survey 1:50,000 sheet 55.

This is a very good area to visit, of enormous interest. Ronald Morris has described all the sites in *The Prehistoric Rock Art of Argyll* (Dolphin, 1977). There is a wide variety of designs, including rosettes, axe heads, spirals and concentric circles, with carvings *in situ* on standing stones, cists and outcrop rock. This is a selection of sites to visit:

Achnabreck 1-3 (NR 8556 9070, 8557 9069, 856950). Large outcrops of rock make this the most extensive site in Britain, with cups, rings and spiral patterns. Begin 350 metres (380 yards) north of the farm, 2.5 kilometres (1½ miles) north-west of Lochgilphead. There is a fenced site in the forest, a second site 140 metres (150 yards) east, and a third just outside the wood.

Ballygowan, Tyness (NR 8161 9778). This fenced site lies 300 metres (330 yards) north of Tyness cottage, 27 metres (30 yards) west of the road. The gritstone slab has fine cups and rings.

61. Achnabreck, Argyll, the largest expanse of carved rock in Britain. The figures are picked out by sunlight on water.

62. Achnabreck, Argyll. A horned spiral is not a common motif.

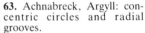

63. Achnabreck, Argyll: concentric circles and radial grooves.

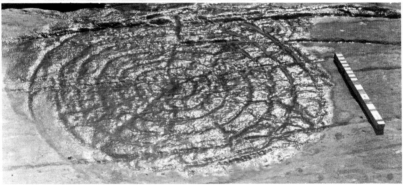

Ballymeanoch (NR 8340 9641). 1 kilometre (⅝ mile) east of Ballymeanoch, 2.5 kilometres (1½ miles) south of Kilmartin, on Killinochinoch Farm, 200 metres (220 yards) west of the main road, are four standing stones and one fallen stone. Three have cup marks and cups and rings.

Cairnbaan 1 and 2 (NR 8387 9105 and 8379 9104). The sites are 350 metres (380 yards) west-southwest of the farm, both fenced. Site 1 is predominantly cups and single grooves, but site 2 has concentric circles, 160 metres (175 yards) west of the first.

Kilmichael Glassary (NR 858935). 100 metres (109 yards) west of the church is a fence enclosing outcrop rock carved with cups of different sizes, some with single or double ducts and a single ring.

64. Cups, rings and grooves at Cairnbaan, Argyll. Some figures are linked.

65. Cups and rings at Ballygowan, Tyness, Argyll.

66. (*Above left*) Temple Wood, Argyll. This spiral is connected to a second on another face of the rock.

67. (*Above right*) A carving at Temple Wood stone circle, Argyll.

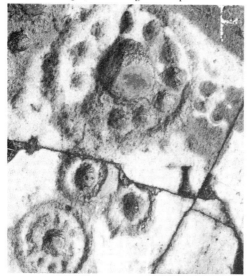

68. (*Left*) A rosette pattern at Ormaig, Argyll. This type appears also in Northumberland. (Photograph: R. W. B. Morris.)

Outside the fence are others, one being carved with concentric circles, cup and duct, different from the rest.

Nether Largie 2 (NR 8309 9847). There is a series of large burial cairns, all interesting to visit, near Kilmartin. This cairn has an open cist with one end covered with large axehead carvings and a cover slab carved with cups and superimposed axeheads.

Nether Largie 3 (NR 8282 9760). 350 metres (380 yards) south-east of Temple Wood in the field is a cup-and-ring marked standing stone, the biggest of a group of four (figure 6).

Ormaig (NR 8222 0267). Much more difficult to reach than those described, this outcrop is the only one in the area to have a 'rosette' design. The carvings are in excellent condition. They are 300 metres (330 yards) south of the farmhouse, 4 kilometres (2½ miles) north of Kilmartin, 55 metres (60 yards) north of the Eas Mor stream and 88 metres (96 yards) east of the road bridge over it. The outcrop is on a steep slope.

Poltalloch (NR 812693). 3.5 kilometres (2¼ miles) south of Kilmartin, 200 metres (220 yards) south-west of a ruined farmhouse, is a fine outcrop slab with cups and rings, one very large figure having four circles around a cup and a V-shaped groove across it.

Ri Cruin (NR 8254 9712). The cairn, signposted, has an open cist with axeheads carved inside (figure 53).

Temple Wood (NR 8263 9783). This circle of standing stones, with horizontal slabs laid between, surrounds burials and is a particularly interesting site. Two of the standing stones have markings, one with two concentric circles, and the other a spiral of six convolutions linked to one of two convolutions on two sides of the same stone.

11
The Glasgow area

Ordnance Survey 1:50,000 sheet 64.

A selection is given. For further details, see Ronald W. B. Morris's *The Prehistoric Rock Art of Southern Scotland* (British Archaeological Reports 86, 1981).

Auchnacraig (NS 5028 7365)
2.5 metres (8 feet) south-west of a house site, there is a gritstone slab near the old stables. There are many cups and some cups and rings, best seen in low light. 65 metres (70 yards) away is another sloping outcrop (NS 5029 7362) with cups and rings, and a third (NS 501730) is 90 metres (100 yards) north-east of 53 Auchnacraig Road, Clydebank. It adjoins the Whitehill group on the next farm, so these easily accessible sites can be visited at the same time.

Glasgow Art Gallery and Museum, Kelvingrove, Glasgow.
There are some good carved stones here.
1. A slab, of unknown provenance, has very well preserved carvings.
2. There are three flat boulders with cups and rings from *Bowling*.
3. A cist cover from *Knappers* (NS 5072 7129), 1.5 kilometres (1 mile) from Clydebank, is unusual and was part of a cist that contained a polished flint axe. Other objects in the 'cemetery' in the sandhill where the cist appeared were bones, pottery, flint and lignite.
4. An interesting slab from *Jedburgh*, found in a garden, has diametric crossed grooves through concentric circles and a ring of cups outside. (Another slab is at Jedburgh Abbey forecourt, NT 651204.)

Greenland Farm
These sites are very rich and important, and easily reached. They are about 1.25 kilometres (¾ mile) north-west of Bowling, and are in grave danger of being destroyed by the farmer.
NS 4344 7460 is 350 metres (380 yards) south of the farm, a prominent smooth gritstone outcrop in boggy ground, and the carvings are some of the best, with a variety of types including

69, 70, 71. Carvings at Greenland Farm, Bowling, Dunbarton-shire. (Photographs: R. W. B. Morris.)

two sets of multiple concentric circles (around cups) that join. NS 4348 7462, a further 50 metres (55 yards) east, has cups and rings, some on a near-vertical face.

Hamilton District Museum, 129 Muir Street, Hamilton.
There is a cist side slab from *Ferniegair,* Chatelherault (NS 7390 5381), which is unusual because it is decorated on two sides and because it seems to be in the Irish passage grave tradition. In the cist was a contracted adult skeleton, well preserved, placed on its side. The cist itself as it is reconstructed in the museum is of sandstone slabs 1.25 by 0.4 metres (4 feet 1 inch by 1 foot 4 inches) internally, with the side-slabs made of grey sandstone 0.25 metres (10 inches) thick.

Other details of the site, part of a bronze age cemetery with four inhumation cists, four urned cremations and a simple inhumation, with finds of a beaker, three food vessels, an enlarged food vessel, an encrusted urn, a cordoned urn, an archer's bracer and vegetable fibre fabric, are given by H. G. Welfare in the *Proceedings of the Society of Antiquaries of Scotland,* volume 106, 1974/5, pages 1-8.

Whitehill
There is a great concentration 3.5 kilometres (2¼ miles) north of Clydebank, but the spectacular Cochno Stone (NS 5045 7385) has been covered to protect it from vandals. Others worth visiting are: NS 5085 7383, 200 metres (220 yards) west of the farm by the road wall: NS 5115 7386, 200 metres (220 yards) north-northeast of the farm in rough pasture by a disused quarry: NS 5130 7398, 370 metres (405 yards) north-northeast of the farm, a domed outcrop beside a footpath: NS 5138 7404, 457 metres (500 yards) north-east of the farm. All these sites are described in detail by Mr Morris.

12
Central Scotland and Fife

Ordnance Survey 1:50,000 sheets 51, 59, 65.

Balbirnie (NO 2850 0304). The monument that the visitor may now see has been moved from its original site 125 metres (137 yards) away because of road widening, and replicas of the carved stones have replaced the originals, now at Edinburgh.

A cairn within a ring of stones, 400 metres (440 yards) from Mains Farms, 1.5 kilometres (1 mile) north-west of Markinch, covered five cists, one of which had carvings on the inside slab. There were cups and cups and rings. Another cist slab had cup marks. A flint knife, jet, beakers, food vessels and cinerary urn sherds came from the cist or scatter.

Castleton. Castleton Farm is 5 kilometres (3 miles) south-southwest of Alloa. There are six outcrop sites around the farm. The carvings vary from a single ring to cups with uninterrupted concentric circles (Grid references: NS 8588 8840; 8851 8831; 8571 8797; 8552 8816; 8555 8811; 8597 8826.)

72. *(Left)* Carvings from Castleton Farm, near Alloa. Scale in decimetres.

73. *(Right)* A carved dolerite slab *(left)* from a cist in the stone circle at Beoch, Ayr, now at the Royal Museums of Scotland, Edinburgh. A slab *(right)* found built into a wall at Glasslie Farm, now at Falkland Palace, Fife.

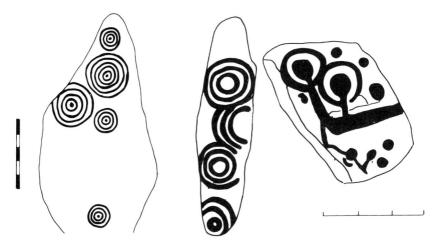

The **Duncroisk** site, near to Killin, is a good site to visit, as there is a cluster of carved rocks 4.5 kilometres (2¾ miles) west-northwest of Killin on a rocky hillock with wide views. There are many cup marks, some with rings, and a solitary example of a ring through which a cross has been cut. (Grid references: NN 5278 3546; 5322 3582; 5313 3588; 5345 3568; 5325 3641.)

Falkland Palace (NO 2507). The museum has three small stones from *East Lomond Hill* and *Glasslie Farm*. An added interest is that these small stones are carved on two faces.

13
Other Scottish sites

The *Proceedings of the Society of Antiquaries of Scotland* has listed many carved rocks. For example, Sutherland, Ross-shire, Inverness, Nairnshire, Elgin, Banff, Aberdeen and Forfarshire had many carvings listed in 1882 on cist covers, stone circles, rock surfaces and boulders. Some were found built into brochs, and some were found in forts.

The *Proceedings* have continued to list such finds, and this is where the reader must look to fill out the picture. The following areas are examples:

Inverness (Ordnance Survey 1:50,000 sheet 26). There are abundant settlements, stone circles and chambered cairns marked on the map, but only two cup-marked stones, at Milton (NH 500 312) and Kinerras (NH 466400).

Loch Rannoch (Ordnance Survey 1:50,000 sheet 42). Sites around Tummel Bridge are marked on the Ordnance Survey map. There are cups and cups and rings at Tullochroisk (NN 712580), Tummel Forest (NN 747611), Tombrech (NN 779566), Braes of Foss (NN 752553) and Garth (NN 757507).

Strathnaver (Ordnance Survey 1:50,000 sheet 10). At the south end of the Kyle of Tongue is a cup-and-ring marked stone (NC 569526) and a cup-marked stone (NC 561526) shown on the Ordnance Survey map.

14
Further reading

General

Haddingham, Evan. *Ancient Carvings in Britain.* Garnstone Press, 1974. (A well presented survey with a useful bibliography.)

Scotland and Northumberland

These areas have been well documented in books that provide details of most sites in a specific area, with illustrations, maps and bibliographies.

Beckensall, Stan. *Northumberland's Prehistoric Rock Carvings.* Pendulum Publications, Rothbury, 1983.

Beckensall, Stan. *The Prehistoric Carved Rocks of Northumberland.* Frank Graham, Newcastle upon Tyne, 1974.

Morris, Ronald. *The Prehistoric Rock Art of Argyll.* Dolphin, 1977.

Morris, Ronald. *The Prehistoric Rock Art of Galloway and the Isle of Man.* Blandford, 1979.

Morris, Ronald. *The Prehistoric Rock Art of Southern Scotland.* British Archaeological Reports Series number 86, 1981.

Other regions have their own specialists working on similar lines and this research may become available soon. Local and national archaeological journals include some items.

Ian and Irene Hewitt of Poole, Dorset, are preparing a complete record of all carvings in the south of England. There are now known to be more carvings than was at first realised.

Acknowledgements

The author is very grateful to all those who have given information, advice and help, and especially to those who have done the fieldwork that has significantly increased our knowledge in recent years. An accurate drawing, map or photograph may involve hours of work and travel, and the author greatly appreciates the efforts of those named in the text who have done this work or made a new discovery. The author particularly acknowledges Mr T. C. Laurie, who acted as guide to the sites on Barningham Moor. The map of Barningham Moor is based on his research.

The author also thanks Mrs Ann Parkin for typing the manuscript with her usual precision.

Index

Page numbers in italic refer to illustrations.